THE UNIVERSAL CHILD
GUIDED BY NATURE
A Montessori Perspective

10TH ANNIVERSARY EDITION

SUSAN MAYCLIN STEPHENSON

II

Joy, feeling one's own value, being appreciated and loved by others, feeling useful and capable of production are all factors of enormous value for the human soul.

—Montessori, *From Childhood to Adolescence*

COVER: These two children are helping each other. One is helping by tying an apron. The other by standing still for a long time to allow the needed practice. It is based on a painting "in the style of Gustav Klimt" by the author.

CONTENTS

INTRODUCTION

In 1963-1964, as a college sophomore, I traveled on the first shipboard university through Europe, North Africa, the Middle East, and Asia. One of the electives I choose was sociology of family life throughout the world.

For more than 50 years now I have found this subject one of the most fascinating, and surely one of the most important, that I have ever encountered. It seems as though I am just beginning to unravel the mysteries of growing up human. So please do not take the ideas presented here as a final word on the subject.

On these pages I will attempt to demonstrate that children all over the world have the same needs in order to thrive, and that these needs are inherent and have been universally observed. Also, I will include some of the topics and specific ideas that have been found useful in teaching others—parents, educators, anyone interested—about Montessori philosophy and practice.

PART 1
THE NEEDS AND TENDENCIES
OF THE UNIVERSAL CHILD

Montessori class in the Tibetan Children's Village (TCV),
Dharamsala, India

A child is indeed universal and the Montessori principles we use in our work have been shown to be valid all over the world. I am going to share with you some of the observations I have made that have convinced me that this is true.

A basic introduction to Montessori work would include the *absorbent mind, the planes (stages) of development*, and a set of universal human urges sometimes called *human needs* or *human tendencies*. I will just focus on a few of the many of these *needs and tendencies* of the universal child that I have observed in many countries. These are exploration, movement, work, maximum effort, perfection, concentration, self-control, communication, belonging, and joy.

There are many ways to explore, depending on the age and stage of development, and all of them are important. Visual exploration can be observed from birth on. A floor bed, in a child's own room or wherever there is room in the home or apartment, supports visual exploration because the child is not looking at the world through the bars of a traditional crib.

Mobiles that move gently on air currents of the room are very valuable for an infant's visual exploration .

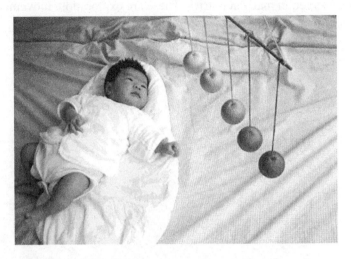

This child in the tiny Himalayan country of Bhutan, by necessity, goes to work with his grandfather and so is able to explore visually a wider world than that of the home.

Although there are drawbacks to this situation, such as limited movement of the child, it certainly provides a rich visual and auditory and social experience.

This Bhutanese child is also able to explore the sounds of the wider world. Auditory exploration began with the voices and the music that the infant heard in the womb.

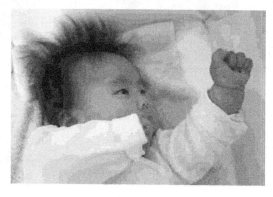

Many of us have noticed how young children tend to put everything in their mouths. That is because tasting begins before birth, and later is an important early way of exploring objects.

Keeping the hands uncovered, and giving freedom of movement in a safe environment is wonderful for the child's exploration by touch.

I took this picture in Bhutan at a very important annual celebration called a *Tsechu*. This child's exploration of fringe was more interesting than beautiful dresses, music, and the dancing, and more important at that moment. No one interrupted her.

From age 0-6, a child wants to be free to be able to safely explore both inside the home and classroom and outside in nature, touching everything.

In the 2nd stage of development the 6-12+ the child explores with the imagination, moving through time and space.

In a class in Canada I questioned these girls—who were building a model of a pyramid—about Egyptian mythology, about *Anubis*, the god who weighs one's heart after death to see if one enters the afterlife or is eaten up by *Ammut*. They knew everything I asked them about; this was not just an art project.

One day I was scanning a picture of an often practiced Montessori birthday celebration during which a child carries a globe around a candle that represents the sun, once for every year of his life and the teacher recites a few sentences for each year.

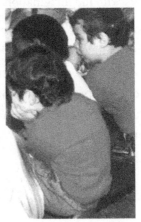

Since it was a picture of our son, I had always focused on him, until this time when the picture was enlarged on my computer! I noticed something shocking. These children were bored!

I realized that with a class of 25-30 children, it is possible to have 25-30 birthday celebrations EACH YEAR!

This helped me understand why in an authentic Montessori primary classroom one almost never sees the traditional preschool "morning group," or any other required collective lesson where children are required to sit for long periods of time listening to an adult instead of moving freely; and it reminded me also of the importance of 1:1 lessons or presentations.

Thinking about this picture made me appreciate the fact that when teaching Montessori 2-6 classes I never scheduled group lessons, and when spontaneous groups formed I never interrupted children's deep concentration on individual work in order to attend.

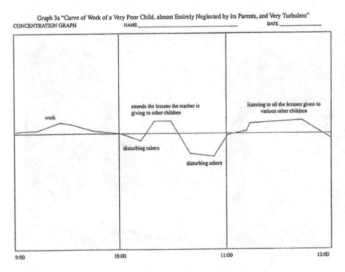

Graph 3a "Curve of Work of a Very Poor Child, almost Entirely Neglected by its Parents, and Very Turbulent"
CONCENTRATION GRAPH   NAME _____   DATE _____

One of the observation tools we use to follow a child's development is a graph of the 3-hour work period from *The Advanced Montessori Method, Volume II.*

"Uninterrupted 3-hour (minimum) free work period" means that there are no required group activities during this time. The child is able to move freely; then we can track individual development of concentration.

In my own teaching I observed, and plotted a graph for one child each day, and after creating one for each child, I plotted a graph for the whole class.

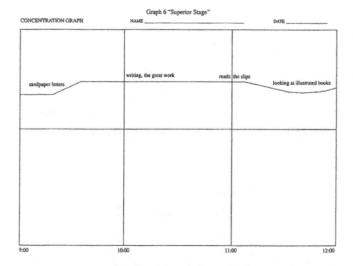

CONCENTRATION GRAPH   Graph 6 "Superior Stage"   NAME _____   DATE _____

sandpaper letters   writing, the great work   reads the slips   looking at illustrated books

9:00   10:00   11:00   12:00

Over the years it was possible to track the improvement in concentration for each child. I shared this information with parents at individual parent meeting and found that parents then began to observe and respect concentration on appropriate activities (NOT screens) at home.

Only with free movement can we see improvement. It is clear in this second graph that this child has come into the room with a plan, perhaps formulated on his way to school or even earlier in the morning. Imagine what would have happened to this impulse to work had he been distracted with required attendance of a group activity.

Of course it is the same for older children and young adults in Montessori environments.

There is a saying: *The teacher is in charge of the minimum, the child the maximum.* This means that we adults provide the environment, link the child to it through lessons, and then get out of the way, because it is from an inner guide that a child will work much more diligently than we can imagine.

Resa is a little girl in Bhutan who I have been able to follow in her development. On my first visit I observed her watching the work of the family from her father's back. Already she was absorbing the way of life, the work of the family. She watched her parents, her grandparents, her older sister, as they carried out their daily work both inside the home and outside.

One day, two years later, as we were leaving the house, we found Resa had gone outside and joined in the sweeping of the courtyard.

This was the real work of the family, caring for the animals, the crops, and keeping the outside area of the family farmhouse organized and clean. She watched her sister and worked just as carefully. It was an example of work, maximum effort, and perfection. It was her choice; one asked her to do it; no one praised or rewarded her.

In a Montessori class in the Torres Strait, north of
Australia, as in classes all over the world—children are quite
serious about real work, here a child is preparing a hard-boiled
egg for a meal.

In a Montessori infant community in Japan, serving oneself sushi with a pair of tongs, and ladling miso soup without spilling a drop, give maximum opportunity to practice perfection of movement.

To aid a child in carrying out real work Dr. Montessori had child-size furniture and tools made to support the child's efforts. Today we can do the same, so children can participate in as much of the real work of the family and the community as possible.

The more precise and careful the lesson by the teacher or parent, the more the child will be able to develop skill in moving, his whole body and his hands.

In observing this child in Bhutan I could tell that he has had a good lesson of rolling the mat and was trying his best to get it perfect.

The next few pages show an example of what we call in the Montessori field *an explosion in the child's development.* This is something that happens in class, often with practical life, language, math, or other work. But it can also happen and be supported in the home.

One day our grandson Tai asked if he could wash the dishes. It was his idea, not ours.

I would say that one of the most important pieces of "Montessori materials" for the home is a stool that allows a child to reach places, and do work, that would otherwise not be possible. And so he began the task.

Then his sister Zahra asked for a turn. She worked tirelessly, scrubbing each piece of cutlery carefully.

Soon they were both working away happily not only on the dishes but also on the kitchen counters.

My job, just as in the classroom, was to watch and see what they needed next as far as materials, and to remove obstacles before they get in the way of concentration and the work.

Zahra noticed crumbs that had fallen to the floor as she "crumbed" the table, and began to sweep them up.

Then she decided to sweep the whole kitchen.

Floor clean, Zahra checked the counters. While Tai continued dishes she washed and polished the counters.

Dishes all washed, Tai began working on their small "child's" table, scrubbing the top, the sides, and the legs.

And then he started cleaning one of the small chairs, in the same careful way.

This kind of sustained, child-initiated, child-directed, purposeful work can occur in many areas of life—in school at home, visiting other family members, and out in the community.

When the children in the first *casa dei bambini* in San Lorenzo, Rome, discovered they could write, they *exploded* into writing, covering every available surface. This was one of the first recorded examples in Montessori's own writing.

No adult can create it or schedule it; we can just introduce it by careful presentations, offer choice to carry out the work in the child's own time and following an interest, support it however possible, and get out of the way.

When an adult suddenly gets inspired to take on a big project, it works to maybe just write it on a "to do" list, or "wait till the week-end."

But when a child at this age suddenly gets inspired to take on a big project, one cannot wait! Children live in the present, they are in the moment and by the weekend they will be interested in something else.

So whenever possible, if we want to see this kind of big work, the resulting mental and physical growth, and the satisfaction and joy that can follow it, we must try to *follow the child* whenever we can.

As I observed the joy of my own grandchildren working in this way, it reminded me of all the times I had seen such wonderful child-centered work explosions in my own teaching years, with children and young adults from age two years to eighteen. But that was years ago.

I wondered if these same kinds of Montessori exciting experiences were still happening in Montessori classes. I wanted to know if it was typical with children in our modern world, in other countries.

My question was soon answered . . .

Some time later I was consulting with a Montessori school, observing in a 3-6 class, in Moscow, Russia. After lunch one of the students started to wash dishes.

Another student got out the table-washing set (seen on the mat on the floor) and began to clean one of the tables. It was common that, after lunch, it was the children who scraped leftovers into the compost bin, washed dishes, swept the floor if needed, and wiped the tables clean so they could be used for working, but today it looked like the beginning of another explosion of child-centered work!

On her own initiative this student cleaned not only the table top, but the edges, and then the sides and legs, just as my grandson had done far away in California.

Then she very happily cleaned the chairs in the same way, humming as she worked. Another student began cleaning the floor with a wet mop.

Perhaps not satisfied with the mop, he got out the window-cleaning squeegee, that seemed to do a better job.

A friend became intrigued with his new floor cleaning system, so he gave her a lesson. And they carried on, cleaning the classroom floor together.

Here they are seen continuing to work on the floor,
another child sweeping, another washing dishes, another child
is cleaning the floor of the language area with a wet mop,
some children still eating their lunch, and some have returned
to other work.

This is a true example of a *casa dei bambini,* a children's house, rather than a school. A place, a home, taken care of by the children.

Montessori *practical life* is more than the wonderful feeling of doing real work, of being helpful to others; this work also sharpens valuable mental skills called *executive functions* of the brain, and are more reliable predictors of academic achievement than IQ scores, and about which more will be mentioned later in this chapter.

Older Children and Young Adults

Adolescents and teenagers in some societies (where young adults are able to work along with adults instead of focusing only on academics and entertainment) are just as likely to choose real work over other activities as younger children.

During the creation of a new Montessori classroom in Bhutan, the son of my host and hostess quite naturally joined us in the work. No one asked him to, he just started working as though it were his role. And no one praised or rewarded him.

In a country school in Thailand the students are in charge of the lawn mowing and maintaining the lawn mower. Why not? Real work is a human need at any age.

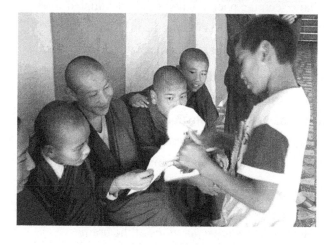

In this boarding school for poor children in Nepal, students begin helping out in all operations of the school as soon as they are able, and by the teenage years are doing the paperwork and sterilizing the medical equipment for an annual USA dental clinic.

I observed a 12-year-old giving adult nuns, who were attending the dental clinic, lessons on brushing their teeth; the nuns did not seem at all surprised at his age or ability.

The universal child wants to *work* and exert *maximum effort*. He wants the results of this work to be as *perfect* as possible.

Executive Functions

I have seen the phenomenon of child-initiated work explosions in Montessori classrooms in all areas of the curriculum, and sometimes in homes with certain toys.

But it is the *practical life real work* that gives the most scope and variety and challenge, and the most valuable results physically, mentally and emotionally. Children love to be mastering the work that they have seen adults doing. This was true in the first *casa dei bambini* in Italy and it is true today.

It has been shown by neuroscientists that certain activities—logical-thinking, multi-step problem-solving, real work—improve *executive functions* of the brain.

Executive functions include skills of working memory, cognitive flexibility, self-control, self-monitoring, planning and prioritizing, inhibitory control, and regulation of emotions.

These skills can be sharpened in certain kinds of sports, dance, and musical studies, when children are inspired to work on their own to reach higher and higher levels of expertise—if their attempts to improve are intrinsically rewarded and not a result of competition, praise, grades, or other external rewards.

This describes how the work is, or should be, carried out in Montessori environments at any age.

It has been shown that providing continued child-centered practice, and continued mastery, of executive function skills is more a predictor of later success and happiness than IQ or other developmental or educational considerations of goals.

All too often older children and young adults are educated in environments, sometimes even Montessori environments, where mastery of an academic curriculum become the central focus instead of executive functions. This can create a throwback to adult-centered assignments and schedules, and destroy true Montessori potential.

What I am sharing with you here—what I have witnessed in places around the world where children and young adults are accepted as valuable contributors to family and society—can insure us that the "universal child" and "the universal adolescent" still exist. We can learn from these international pockets of potential.

When we focus on and respect—at every stage of life—real work that is necessary to the social group, we support the development of concentration and happiness.

This gives the older child and young adult a feeling of belonging and contributing, knowledge of themselves and others, and a confidence to experiment, collaborate, and think outside the box to solve problems.

Sharpening executive functions will go a long way to prepare them for challenges in a future in what we all know is a unpredictable.

The Need for Concentration

Just as with the universal need for real work, we are now beginning to understand— through scientific proof—the mental, physical, and emotional benefits of focusing in the present moment, meditating, concentrating without being interrupted.

We adults must carve out a time and place. But in a true Montessori environment focus and concentration are carried out many hours of each day, not by sitting still, but through movement and work.

An example is this young child in an infant community (age 1-2.5) in Sweden. It is clear in the body language and the facial expression that this child is concentrating.

It is often the adults' role to provide activities that engage the child's hand and mind working together on purposeful work appropriate to the child's interest and stage of development, but sometimes children discover their own work.

These boys in a school playground in Bhutan choose to concentrate on trying to fix the sidewalk rather than playing on the climbing structures.

The most successful activities engage the child's hand and mind working together, activities with a real purpose, such as sewing in this classroom in Thailand. These purposeful activities are the ones that call forth deep concentration.

Activities such as learning to read words, and read music, as well as many other academic challenges, inspire concentration of a very high level and should not be interrupted until the child is finished with the chosen work.

The picture on the next page is a student in one of my own Montessori 6-12 classes.

After reading the music on the Montessori bells she wrote her own composition on a piece of paper—making the staff lines with a ruler—then played it on the bells. Other students in this class wrote music for each other to play on the bells and on the piano.

It is often the case that Montessori teachers follow the practice of an uninterrupted child-centered 3-hour minimum "work period" each morning, and sometimes again in the afternoon.

But sometimes, for a variety of different reasons, Montessori teachers of older children and young adults find themselves forced to teach in the traditional TCC (adult or text centered) factory-model way: making assignments and schedules, and reverting to hour-long work periods in order to cover an adult-dictated (Montessori or traditional) curriculum.

For myself today, as I try to eliminate obstacles to my own creative work which means a "flow" day of writing and painting, cooking, gardening or playing piano—and in years past overseeing a Montessori primary or elementary class—I would never be able to concentrate or be productive if I had to think about one-hour work periods; and I never required this of my students, who ranged from 2-18years.

One of the joys of Montessori teaching is that one never knows what each child will have worked on each day—what amazing solution or conclusion or individual or group assignment they will have designed, worked on, or mastered— till the day ended.

I hope this book is helpful to adults who feel a need for support in trusting children to work, to concentrate, to create, and as a result to be kind and happy.

When the children had completed an absorbing bit of work, they appeared rested and deeply pleased. It almost seemed as if a road had opened up within their souls that led to all their latent powers, revealing the better part of themselves. They exhibited a great affability to everyone, put themselves out to help others, and seemed full of good will.

It was clear to me that the concept of order and the development of character, of the intellectual and emotional life, must derive from this veiled source. Thereafter, I set out to find experimental objects that would make this concentration possible, and carefully worked out an environment that would present the most favorable external conditions for this concentration. And that is how my method began.

— Montessori, *The Child in the Family*

Control of one's physical movements is the beginning of mental and emotional control. Self-control cannot develop unless a child is in charge of himself and his movements, free of control by another.

This can begin very early in life if a child is supported in his efforts. Learning to act independently, to wait until someone is finished with something till he can use it, learning to respect and not interrupt someone who is concentrating, all strengthen abilities to control motivation and action.

Montessori did not invent *walking on the line*, which is a daily individual activity found in Montessori classes; her genius was in making this natural impulse to learn to control one's body, to master balance, a method of teaching a child to walk carefully in the classroom. The teacher does not tell a child to "Stop running," because the many *walking on the line* challenges teach carefully walking, "teaching by teaching instead of by correcting."

This young girl is walking on the line in a Montessori class in Moscow.

And the teacher is modeling a further challenge in control of movement for another child who can scarcely believe how careful the teacher is walking—the bell she is carrying is completely silent! This child is squatting down to see if it truly is a bell that could make a sound. No doubt he then accepted the challenge to walk just as carefully and quietly himself.

In a traditional school in a village in Thailand I saw a variation on the natural instinct to learn to control one's movement, to improve the skill of balance. This child was walking on two coconut halves held by a rope. Ingenious.

This practice physical control is available to any child at any time in a primary Montessori classroom and sometimes appears to be almost a walking meditation. I have often observed a child, at work at a table—perhaps having reached a challenging part—get up and go to the line, walk silently for a few minutes, then return to the work refreshed, meeting the challenge with vigor.

Through all of the stages covered thus far it is clear that the child is becoming, more and more, a part of the family, the class, or other social group. This acceptance and participation, this belonging, is vital to healthy physical, mental, and emotional development.

Communication (which will have a section all on its own later in this book) is connected with all learning and living.

And as we see over and over, the child's uninterrupted concentration—on developmentally helpful and healthy work—is a clear path to joy.

PART 2
SHARING MONTESSORI
WITH THE WORLD

Finding Out What "Montessori" Means

It is an important goal for many reasons that children be educated by people from their own country, from their own culture. Children should know that the adults from their own place are as capable as anyone else.

However, until that is possible, there are many ways to share. Many people today know that there is something special about this system of education called *Montessori*. First of all I always try to discover what Montessori means to those I will be working with.

During my first trip to Bhutan, my hostess and I traveled far into the hills outside of the capital of Thimphu, getting lost more than once, to a Buddhist monastery where we had heard there were Montessori classes.

But when we arrived, we found a typical "chalk and talk" class (where the teacher teaches by talking and writing on the blackboard and the children copy what he or she has written.)

I thought hard about this as we watched the children sitting very quietly and diligently copying from the blackboard. I did not want to invalidate what the teacher was doing but sincerely wanted to know why this class was known as a Montessori class.

Finally I asked the teacher which of the Montessori elements he had found the most helpful, and he replied, "We do not hit the children in our Montessori school."

Certainly it is true that treating children more gently, in the name of "Montessori," is a good start in countries where discipline is commonly enforced by physical punishment.

By contrast, at the Tibetan Children's Village in Dharamsala, India, where the teaching began many years ago with AMI teacher trainer Abs Joosten, a Dutch man who had studied closely with Montessori, I found quite good classes.

Here the word *Montessori* means what we hope for, well-trained teachers, children concentrating and engaged in their work, enjoying learning, and being helpful and kind to one another.

In a school in Nepal, the teacher had taken a very short Montessori training course with no supervised practice with materials, no album or materials making, no authentic Montessori classroom to observe and student teach. Observations. So the teacher did not know how to create a Montessori environment, or give 1:1 presentations, etc.

Here, as in many places in the world, the idea *Montessori* meant that children did not have to sit in chairs, but the idea of "follow the child" was very misunderstood. However, children having freedom to move about and explore the room and talk to each other could be considered a good place to begin.

In Bhutan there were just three fully trained AMI teachers in the whole country, so we tried to make it possible for the teacher to visit, as a start in understanding Montessori. I gave public lectures, and years later returned with my daughter to help set up the first true Montessori classroom, and guide the newly trained AMI teacher through her first days.

In Dharamsala, India where the Dalai Lama began the Montessori program many years ago, there is continued work to raise the standards of the Montessori teachers, some by my good friend Lhamo Pemba, the first AMI Tibetan-Bhutanese Montessori teacher trainer.

And in this class in Nepal, the next step was to gather funds and support for Montessori teacher training.

A Canadian couple who are good friends of one of the directors of SMD (Sri Mangal Dvip) boarding school in Kathmandu, Nepal (the classroom pictured on the last page) sponsored two traditional teachers to take the 9-month, full time AMI primary Montessori training at The Navadisha Foundation in Chennai, India. They returned to begin the establishment of true Montessori classes.

RESEARCHING A CULTURE
IN PREPARATION FOR SHARING MONTESSORI

One of the golden rules in Montessori is that we prepare
children to adapt to *their own time and place.*

So after finding out what kind of Montessori already
exists in a country or area where one hopes to share what one
knows about Montessori, it is very important to learn all one
can about that place. Every country, every culture has a unique
character, strengths and weaknesses, gifts and needs. And just
as a teacher begins by getting to know the child, one must
begin by getting to know the history and culture of the country.

Water plays a large part in the practical life work of a
Montessori classroom. But in Bhutan because the traditional
farmhouse is made of pounded mud walls with a wide roof to

protect them from dissolving in the rain, and there is no running water inside the home; bathing, laundry, all water-related activities are carried on outside the house.

So how does one wash hands before a meal? I asked for a lesson.

 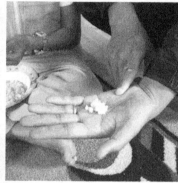

Rice is served at every meal, so one first takes a bit of rice into one's hand.

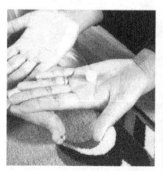 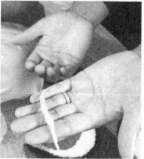

Then it is rolled into a ball, then a "snake," and then, finally, rubbed all over the hands to clean them, front and back.

Next this little cleaning ball of rice is then used to pick up any dirt or dust that one might find on the clothing. Then it is laid aside as one picks up fresh rice, with clean fingers, and begins the meal.

Even if children in Bhutan learn the Western way of eating with a spoon, fork, and knife, seated on a chair at a table, it is important they practice, and respect, the traditions of eating with one's hands while being seated on the floor.

What about washing clothing? Water is at a premium in many places in the world.

At The Tibetan children's village in Dharamsala, India, the taps are turned on each morning and water from the melting Himalayan snow fills the large black tanks on the roofs of buildings. This boy is washing his socks with water from the tank on the roof of his home.

We must learn what the languages of the country are.

It is important to know at what age children are expected to know which languages if we want to develop a primary class Montessori language program with oral language lessons, sandpaper letters, movable alphabets, grammar and sentence analysis material, etc.

In the SMD school in Nepal mentioned earlier, children do their work daily in three languages: Hindi, Tibetan, and English. So how do we do Montessori?

There is research going on today about how to manage to retain independence in a Montessori class when children are expected to master three languages.

Here is the main difficulty. It is important that children be exposed to the best of a language by hearing a native speaker, but too many adults in a Montessori class can cause major problems.

With a well-trained and experienced primary teacher for example, the optimum ratio recommended by Montessori is one trained teacher to 30-35 children from age 2-6, with one non-teaching assistant. With too many adults, who naturally want to be kept occupied and helpful, children can lose the ability to solve problems on their own, or to go to other children for help, or to help and teach other children.

We will see what is discovered with this research,

I grew up in the US during the *cold war* when there was very little communication with the Soviet Union. We heard strange stories about a cold, dark, colorless country with no beauty. Now that there is a resurgence of Montessori in Russia and other countries in this part of the world I welcomed the opportunity to learn about, and work with a Montessori school in Moscow.

No beauty? No culture? Wrong. I discovered that the Imperial Ballet of the Russia Empire was founded in the 1740's, before we in the USA even had a country!

When I attended the ballet *The Sleeping Beauty* at the Kremlin in Moscow two young girls in front of me danced throughout, and no one seemed to mind their expression of the music; no one told them to sit down.

I visited the village of Tchaikovsky where his countrymen, even more than tourists, regularly tour his home and celebrate his music; it seemed that celebrating music and dance was an everyday affair.

Appreciation of arts was evident everywhere I went in Russia. Here at home we certainly have the arts and culture, but since the United States is a melting pot of cultures, it is not so common to see people appreciating European and Eastern European cultures such as I observed, and enjoyed, there.

The line of local Russian people waiting for the art museum to open stretched around the block in the middle of the week, in the morning, on a cold day, for no special exhibit, just art.

Traditional crafts were evident in the classrooms as containers for language materials, and there were many children's books available about the arts.

In researching the cultures of Thailand I found that meditation was the common way to begin class in non-Montessori schools, and some families meditate together in the evening, focusing on becoming a better person.

Seated meditation, assigned by an adult, is not carried out in Montessori schools because deep concentration and mindfulness occur naturally when a child is working on appropriate tasks. But it was very appropriate in this school, in this culture.

In preparation for the first AMI 3-6 teacher training course in Thailand I gave a few lectures and interviews. One day as I was giving a talk on the value of uninterrupted concentration I kept hearing the translator use the word *samadhi* which I later found means *meditation* or *concentration*.

So the value of uninterrupted concentration in Montessori classes was very easy to explain in this country.

The Montessori lessons on *grace and courtesy* were also easy to explain in this culture. Below is a page from a textbook on this subject in Thailand. In the picture two children are practicing the tradition of keeping one's head lower than that of an older person.

นิดและหน่อยอยากเดินไปหยิบของให้
เพื่อน แต่ไม่กล้าเดินผ่านคุณครูที่นั่งอยู่ที่เก้าอี้

During my presentation, at an annual AMI international congress where I showed this picture, there was a question, "Is this lowering of the head in respect common in other countries?"

Several people in the audience, each from a different Asian country, assured us that this was still common practice.

It is clear that learning about these customs is very valuable in preparation for sharing our knowledge of Montessori education around the world.

Explaining Montessori

Montessori education is action; it is a way of living. It is not dependent on expensive special materials and the principles can sometimes be observed in daily life if we know what to look for. It is svery helpful when we can explain Montessori through the actions of children rather than by mere words. An example was the young adults in charge of the dental clinic and teaching tooth-brushing in Nepal. Here is an example of how I was able to explain this in Bhutan.

It was during my first trip to this beautiful Himalayan country. Sitting with a group of traditional teachers who were very interested in learning more about Montessori, and wanting to find out what they could use in their own traditional classes of children from age 3-9, I was attempting to explain the value of real, purposeful work and concentration, and the results we see in children when this child-chosen work and concentration is not interrupted.

As the meeting ended, and I admit I had not been able to make my message clear, my translator was helping me answer questions. Several of us stood talking at the door of the class where we were preparing to leave, when I noticed the son of one of the teachers beginning to stack the red and orange plastic chairs that we had been sitting on, stacking them in two piles, the way he knew they should be put away.

But, as we were still busy and the chairs were now stacked, he began unstacking them. We watched. I asked the teachers to stand quietly with me at the entrance to the classroom, to observe to see what would happen next.

First he had stacked them in two piles, one red and one orange. Then the young boy unstacked and restacked the chairs, creating a pattern of alternating three of each color, three red and then three orange and then three red chairs. Then he unstacked them again.

This time he again made two stacks, alternating single red and single orange, but then he began a third pile, starting over with three stacks of alternating colors.

Before each stacking, each artistic/mathematical creation, the child stood looking at the chairs for a moment, possibly creating the next pattern in his mind.

At one point it became clear that he was finished, satisfied with his creation. He did not look at an adult for validation, praise, or approval; in fact sometimes such adult input can even reduce the child's satisfaction with effort and work.

The teachers realized the value of leaving the child to his work until he was satisfied, till he had reached a goal only he understood, till the work was done. And it was an excellent example of what can happen when the work is not interrupted.

I was then able to talk about the value of carrying out real work, of contributing to the group, about the mind and the body working together toward an intelligent purpose, and even the natural mathematical mind and how creating patterns is a function of the human brain from a very early age.

We did not leave at the scheduled time, but ours became an enlightening conversation, with the teachers contributing their own examples. This child was far more successful in exemplifying Montessori, by means of his actions, his concentration, and resulting happiness, than ever could have been done with mere words.

MENTORING A NEW MONTESSORI TEACHER

When one is an experienced Montessori teacher, knowledgeable about the culture, and the adaptations that will be needed in introducing these idea in a new place, mentoring is an excellent way to share and explain Montessori.

This next example was during my third trip to Bhutan, this time with my daughter who is also AMI Montessori 0-3, 3-6, and 6-12 teacher educated.

When we arrived this is what the tiny classroom was like. There were a few materials in the back of the room, but the walls were covered with the traditional teaching aids. The windows were covered, perhaps to prevent distractions, and the children were required to sit at tables and follow the instructions of the teacher. The teacher was not Montessori trained. The head of the school had earned an AMI diploma on the first primary course in Thailand, but was also head of the school and unable to be in the classroom full time so she was trying to teach Montessori to the traditional teacher.

Thanks to two USA schools we brought some materials and money to have more made locally.

Children learn from the environment instead of directly from the teacher, so creating the environment that attracted the children was our first priority. We cleared the walls, uncovered the windows and several people volunteered to help clean and paint.

Practical life materials must reflect, not our culture back in the USA, but the life the children have grown up seeing around them. Here you see a traditional broom that we discovered was being used everywhere, inside and out. So we asked the broom maker to take one apart and create two child-size brooms in the same style.

The dressing frame we had made were simple wooden frames with lovely traditional Bhutanese fabric. Then we researched what kind of clothing fastenings are used in this culture because the clothing is unique. Because the Bhutanese do not have ribbon like we would use for the tying frame at home, we used men's boot laces.

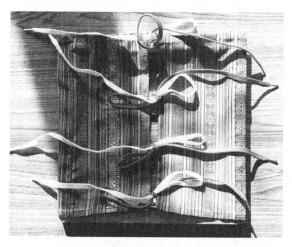

My daughter made vocabulary cards from Bhutanese children's picture books found in a bookstore in the capitol.

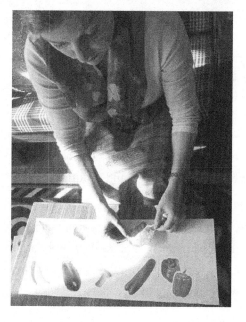

First, for the vocabulary cards, and for the art to be hung on the wall, we looked for pictures of items from the children's culture and country and then those of the wider world.

Wanting to paint the elegant black window trim we learned that it is not paint that is used, but a special rock that is soaked overnight and then applied like whitewash.

There were no shelves or cupboards so we had a few made. You can see the sandpaper letters displayed in front of the beautiful, now uncovered, windows. The best floor mats available in the country were small and beautiful Tibetan carpets.

Amazingly we found a few Montessori *number rods* in the school that could be painted, and used as a model for making the rest; they were being used as "pointers" (to the blackboards or wall charts) by the teachers.

In storage we discovered both a binomial and trinomial cube, badly in need of paint. There was only one shade of yellow paint in the town and it matched perfectly.

Here you can see my daughter Narda huddled next to the heater to help dry the paint, accompanied by my hostess' son Kinley who had already worked on painting the walls, and was ready to help in any way.

We had had a few tables made, and some stools as making chairs was out of the question; we were trying to avoid plastic as much as possible and the only chairs, and almost all of the practical life materials, were made of plastic as Bhutan is gradually entering the "modern" world and importing household goods from India and China.

Soon the room was ready, as much as it could be. Clean, bright, a "line" for walking on the line made with green tape, a few practical life activities, floor and table mats.

The room was tiny, but very much "Montessori" by the time we finished.

The next morning the children would come. Just as with any new class there were small group activities combined with 1:1 lessons or invitations to choose something from the shelf. The traditional teacher led songs and read stories, while I encouraged Dendy, the AMI teacher—for whom this was the first real "Montessori" day—to invite children one at a time to select something from the shelf and take it to a table or a floor mat.

I mentored the teacher for three days, gradually moving more and more into the background and trying to be invisible. Each child was invited to come into the room, pick a table or floor mat to mark his work space, and then to select something to work on. Suddenly I looked up and noticed several of the parents looking in at a window next to the entrance. Later we discovered that they were amazed, unbelieving of how calm and focused their children were behaving in the new environment.

There were many languages represented in this school. This little boy cried himself to sleep the first day, we think because no one spoke his language and could not explain anything to him. At the end of the first morning he ended up sleeping in the book corner.

In the afternoon he sat on the assistant's lap (the traditional teacher who led the small groups) and watched the other children as they learned how to choose work, use it, and put it away. He figured it out and in the morning of the second day he came into the room, got out a table mat, took one of the sorting activities to a table, and started working.

On the third day, when he saw that another child had dropped a bead from the bead-stringing work, and it had rolled across the room, he was quick to get up from his own work and retrieve it for her.

This kind of progress would not have been possible had this been a school where children are required to sit still in a group and learn from the teacher's words. It is the miracle of the universal child, guided by nature.

PART 3
THE UNIVERSAL CHILD GROWS UP

WE ALL HAVE NEEDS

We have looked at some of the universal human needs from the perspective of the universal child. However all of us were at one time universal children, and as adults we still have these needs, just met in different ways.

What are the needs that the adult and the child have in common?

Aside from the human *needs and tendencies* that have been discussed in this book, Silvana Montanaro, MD, one of the first Assistant to Infancy teacher trainers, speaks of two other needs that she calls the *two psychological legs*. She tells us that when they are strong, so are we.

The first *psychological leg* is strengthened by meeting the need to feel loved and safe and cared for, to feel that the world is a good place, that our needs will always be taken care of. In the Assistants to Infancy, 0-3, course, one learns that this need is met by gentle handling and soft voice, by responding to the child quickly. One learns to observe carefully in order to know as much about each unique infant and how to provide what is needed.

As the teacher is doing at the Buddhist altar in this Montessori class at the Tibetan Children's Village in India, creating a safe and loving place for children can help an adult also feel safe and loved.

I have seen the same attitude at classroom altars in schools in Thailand. Children cut and arrange the flowers, light the incense, clean and care for the altar and—just as in this classroom in India—learn to pray for the happiness for others.

I have also seen small Christian altars in Montessori classrooms high in the Andes mountains in Peru, and in a non-denominational class in the USA, where the "altar" is more of a nature table, containing a shell and a vase of flowers, inviting the children to care for nature. These emotions of empathy and compassion are shared by children and adults.

The second *psychological leg* is trust in oneself. We all, children and adults, want unconditional love, we want to love ourselves and be loved just as we are.

There are many ways we help the very youngest children learn that they are okay just as they are. Time to exercise physical abilities, unrushed to learn to turn over, reach, push-up, crawl, etc. gives a message that "you are fine just the way you are." A child who is allowed uninterrupted time for purposeful work suited to his stage of development, and who is not rushed or compared with others, can develop a good feeling about himself, can love himself just as he is.

These children are not in "walkers," or being held up to practice walking on the adult schedule, or always being carried. There is no rush. They are free to pull-up on bars, to cruise and stand and get down, at just the right time, for just the right amount of time; to practice walking by pushing a stroller, and trusted to learn to go up and down stairs.

There are many ways we help the very youngest children learn that they are okay just as they are. A child who is not rushed or compared with others, can develop a good feeling about himself, can love himself just as he is. That is a strong 2nd psychological leg.

How do we adults learn to love ourselves just the way we are? It is not by comparing ourselves with others, trying to be more beautiful or by having more stuff or leisure time, or being proud of being overworked, as the media might have us believe.

Like children, we also want to explore, learn, to carry out important work, to concentrate, to develop self-control, and when we achieve this balance, express our happiness by helping others.

But do we have to make a list and always be thinking about the next thing?

In Bhutan I asked the father of my hostess's family to show me how to make traditional steamed *momos*. The two children joined in without being asked. It was like they were with us in the moment just waiting to participate and help.

In Thailand I have seen simple (or elaborate) structures called *salas*. They are for sitting, thinking, being—and it is acceptable to do this! It was a new idea for me but I try to tell myself now and then it is okay just to be in the moment, to pay attention to what I am doing right now, instead of rushing to do the next thing. That I am okay just the way I am, right now. That is trust in myself, loving myself, the second *psychological leg*, and I want mine to be strong.

Then I can be working like the children in a Montessori class, completely involved with what I am doing, and maybe with the same results. As Montessori observed the result of concentration on appropriate work in the moment . . . *a road had opened up within their souls that led to all their latent powers, revealing the better part of themselves. They exhibited a great affability to everyone, put themselves out to help others, and seemed full of good will.*

In the Montessori field we are fortunate to have never-ending satisfying work, continually learning about being parents and teachers. The adult students in the previous picture practice with materials for many weeks in order to know how de,pmstrate each, to give a lesson. They will be able to observe and assess when each child is ready for a 1:1 lesson on a piece of material, which required being totally in the moment. And then will be completely involved with that lesson. Parents get to share their daily lives with ever-changing children, and can also learn to observe, to look for an interest.

We constantly get to learn new things in all areas of knowledge, and use our hands and bodies to become better and better at what we do.

We get to help children learn, with no pressure to grade or compare, just satisfaction for a job well done. And when we see how well this attitude toward being, and learning, works so well for others, maybe we can learn to have it for ourselves.

Here is a picture of me (second from the left) having dinner with Montessori teachers and administrators and teacher trainers in Moscow, Russia. It reminds me of how lucky we are in the Montessori world to be able to discuss life, and children, and human development, and happiness, with some of the most wonderful, hopeful, and supportive people on earth.

What a wonderful way to grow, learn, and feel good about oneself.

Communication as a subject has appeared in many places throughout this book, but here I would like to give it a bit more attention because it is so important for children and adults, at home, in the Montessori school community, in life.

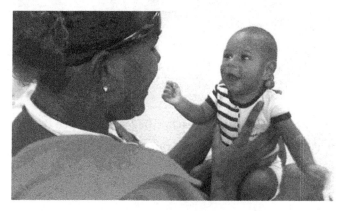

We see that language is more than words when a child mirrors our facial expressions and emotions.

Listening is at least as important as speaking. In communication between ourselves and children, and in communicating about Montessori, we are often focused on the "expert", meaning the adult, or the Montessori speaker.

But the child, and the person wanting to learn about Montessori, have as much to teach us as we have to teach them. Practicing patience and humility, and listening carefully, all help establish true communication.

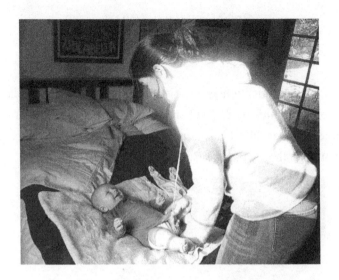

Communication can be established and enriched during every daily activity in the beginning of life.

green anemone

Learning about the world cannot come from pictures or books, until one has learned that these images represent something real that can be experienced through the senses. And the richer that experience is, using as many senses as possible, the more solid the learning.

Imagine that a parent is passionate about life in the tide pools on the coast, and can hardly wait to share this interest with a child. For example, imagine the quality of learning that takes place when a child is shown a picture of an *anemone* and then immediately given the word. It would mean very little to a child new to the concept of tide pool life,

There is a saying that summarizes a phenomenon observed daily in Montessori environments, when movement, hearing, touching, seeing, tasting, smelling . . . are experienced simultaneously, "neurons that fire together, wire together." (Hebb's Law). True learning occurs.

Now imagine an experience of, and learning the name of, *anemone* beginning with a walk on the beach, the smell of salt water from the sea, the call of a seagull, the cool breeze, and maybe a little heat on one's face from the morning sun.

Imagine a child discovering a tide pool containing many different life forms, vegetable and animal, barnacles, starfish, mussels, anemones, and asking, "Can I touch?

The silence and green glow of two open green anemones. Reaching toward an anemone as the incoming tide tickles her feet, and feeling the tentacles gently closing around her finger.

And imagine what the word *anemone* will now mean to this child, and how much more meaningful the picture and label will be. True knowledge is based on experience, not on words.

As Audrey Sillick says in the article "Sowing the Seeds of the Sciences: Our Gift to the Future" (NAMTA publication *Montessori Voices: Guided by Nature*):

Once we know the word *for something there is a tendency to think that we know that thing.*

green anemone

But when the knowledge of the word, or the label or name, is based on experience one can abstract that other pictures or words are based on real objects.

That father passionate about marine life can now show the child pictures of items that cannot be experienced, and the pictures will mean something.

How does this apply to communicating about, and understanding what the word *Montessori* means?

Over the years I have seen many examples of the word Montessori being used when there has been no real experience. Just as with my example of trying to explain Montessori to the teachers in Bhutan, it was not my words but it was being able to observe a child intent and deeply concentrating on his work of making patterns with stacks of red and orange chairs. And it was the parents looking in the window at the first Montessori days in that country, that helped them understand just what the word *Montessori* can stand for.

Here is another example:

A winter walk in the woods, the mother following the speed and interests of the child, never knowing what will grab his attention next, when he will stop to explore.

The squish sound and feel of walking through mud, the smell of fresh damp air.

Being quiet and so focused on the surrounding many shades of green: the grass, the pine needles, the tree leaves, lichen, and moss-covered tree trunks.

The child discovers the soft feel of something like a fuzzy carpet on the trunk of a tree.

Discovering that the same soft fuzz is growing on the tree roots that have emerged from the ground, and on all of the tree trunks within reach . . . touching . . . touching . . .

After all of this experience he finally asks, "What is this?" And only then the mother gives him the word, *moss*.

moss

Now he has work to do—again touching all of the moss he can find but now naming it. Later a picture will bring back all of these memories; he will always know *moss*.

Communicating about Montessori is the same. It cannot be done by words, lectures, or books alone. Montessori can only truly be understood through a wealth of varied experiences, conscious parenting, years working in the classroom (as has the teacher in this school in Moscow), and experience in explaining, and continuing to learn about, Montessori.

Communicating about Montessori works when one's speaking and sharing (and writing) is based on good Montessori teacher training, positive teaching experience, listening, learning about the needs of the family and culture, talking and laughing together, being humble, exploring together in both the most privileged and simple homes and classrooms, all of us working together for the good of the child and the future of humankind.

PART 4 –
WE ARE ALL
GUIDED BY NATURE

I think we are very lucky that our work is not an artificial creation by adults imposed upon unwilling children.

Our support of the development of the universal child is, above all, guided by nature, and the natural instincts that we are all born with, to create a healthy and happy life for ourselves and others. Being surrounded by, and learning about plants and animals, is instructive and healthy for all.

Children are naturally attracted to nature; this young child spent a lot of time being held up by a patient dad in order to watch fish silently move through the water in an aquarium . . .

We can help children, whenever possible, to learn where the food we eat actually comes from. I remember well my grandson reaching for his first garden-grown strawberry. He loved eating fruit of all kinds, especially berries, but had not yet seen them growing on a plant. He couldn't figure out what was happening when he tried to pick it up, what was holding it to the plant.

"Hmm, why is this strawberry stuck to the plant? Why can't I just pick it up?" were his questions, with a slightly frustrating look on his face.

Then he learned how to pick the strawberries carefully, and he appreciated how delicious they are when eaten just after being picked. He became the first one to volunteer to pick the strawberries and blueberries.

It is in the nature of a child to want to learn to touch nature, such as this starfish in a tide pool, gently and with respect, as he himself has been treated.

Just as with all of the real daily work of the family, caring for plants, and gardening are important for the growing child. It doesn't have to be a garden but could be just a house plant that needs to be watered, and kept clean, gives opportunity to learn about the needs of plants through observation and their care. When a child learns about the basic physical needs of a plant for example—warmth, light, water, nutrients (from the soil or hydroponics)—opens the door to an awareness of the physical needs of animals, including humans. And later the mental, emotional, and spiritual needs, all guided by nature.

Our own attitudes, as parents and teachers, toward plants and animals is a very important part of a child's education about nature; we are their most important models.

Exploring the countryside, the shore, fields, mountains, the town, for "weeds," grasses, and wildflowers—that sometimes push themselves through the cracks in sidewalks to meet their needs—provides excellent lessons in nature.

Understanding that humans are needed sometimes to help plants grow can inspire children to work hard to care for them in the home and school.

This child, in a classroom that is part of the AMI Montessori Initiative in the Torres Strait Indigenous communities of Australia, is caring for the school banana plant.

To link the home or classroom to nature in all seasons, a "nature table" or "nature shelf" provides a place for those gathered treasures that can then be studied, drawn, shared.

The above picture is from a primary classroom in Moscow, Russia, but fall leaves and pinecones are found during the fall season in classrooms around the world.

A pond in this country school in Thailand provides ample opportunity for learning about the needs of plants and animals, and more importantly, the chance to take care of plants and animals.

In Bhutan, in preparation for the coronation of the new king in 2008, what did the children do? Did they go shopping? Buy new clothing? Well maybe they did . . . But they also cleaned up their precious natural environment, in towns and villages throughout the country.

Based on what has been observed in the Montessori world over the last 100 years it seems quite probable that a human being is born with all of the wisdom necessary to create a better world. These include the ability to create a physical, mental, and emotional balance for oneself, a love for the natural world and the earth and the desire to protect it, and a compassion for other humans.

Our history, our roots, are deep and strong and reach around the world. We are united, like the rings of a tree trunk, around a central core, and that core is the practice of Montessori, and exact and joyful effort with our children. Our branches lift the children up toward the stars, toward the harmony of the universe.

—Karin Salzmann at the 1992 /USA Summer Institute

As we continue with our work as parents, teachers, supporters of the natural development of the universal child, and the universal adult, guided by nature, let us keep in mind these words of Dr. Montessori:

Education should not limit itself to seeking new methods for a mostly arid transmission of knowledge: its aim must be to give the necessary aid to human development.

   —*From Childhood to Adolescence*

The child is capable of developing and giving us tangible proof of the possibility of a better humanity. He has shown us the true process of construction of the human being. We have seen children totally change as they acquire a love for things and as their sense of order, discipline, and self-control develops within them.... The child is both a hope and a promise for mankind.

   — *Education and Peace*

We then become witnesses to the development of the human soul; the emergence of the New Man, who will no longer be the victim of events but, thanks to his clarity of vision, will become able to direct and to mosld the future of mankind.

   — *The Absorbent Mind*

MONTESSORI AUTHENTICITY

The word *Montessori* is legally unprotected and in the public domain; as a result it can be used to label educational materials, schools, and teacher training courses that are not based on authentic Montessori principles and practice.

In the years after many people came to the slums of Rome to see the "miracle" children, Montessori's ideas began to spread around the world. In 1929, after this first massive spread of "Montessori" practice, Dr. Montessori realized that there needed to be a way to help people maintain the high standards that everyone hoped for. To do this she formed the Association Montessori Internationale (AMI).

The purpose of this international organization, headquartered in Amsterdam, is not to judge or criticize attempts to practice Montessori at home, to train teachers, or to create Montessori environments; it is to be there, when help is requested, no matter the level of progress.

Here are a few of the many ways AMI helps people:

(1) Continually assess and improve the multi-year education program (TOT, Training of Trainers) whereby experienced AMI teachers become teacher trainers

(2) Continually assess and improve teacher education courses, exam questions, training of examiners, and helping teachers to begin their work

(3) Support research on why Montessori practice works, collaboration with neuroscientists, psychologist, medical doctors, and specialists in others fields.

(4) Outreach to help teachers, parents, administrators, children —in Montessori schools, and where complete AMI teacher training is not possible: orphanages, refugee camps, traditional schools, and more.

I have been very fortunate, because of my wonderful teacher training and successful, joyful, years in the classroom with children and young adults from 2-18 years, to be able to help in all of these ways—helping parents, teachers, administrators, government officials, university professors and students, etc., in over 30 countries.

Sometimes "a little Montessori" is helpful, but that depends on which part. There is a saying, "One can find authentic Montessori practice with no materials, but not without a well-trained Montessori teacher." My focus is to help parents and teachers, because then they will be able to create the correct environments for children on their own.

Authentic Montessori practice is scientific, based on over 100 years to research all over the world. In my own experience No matter where one is on this journey, there always a way to help a parent or teacher, "take the next step" in following Montessori ideas. This is why I continue to consult, speak, and write.

For AMI (Association Montessori Internationale) information: www.montessori-ami.org

THE AUTHOR

Susan has been working in the Montessori field for fifty-two years in more than thirty countries, first as a mother, then as a teacher, school administrator, school consultant, speaker at Montessori and other conferences, at universities and for governments. She lectures and serves as an oral examiner for AMI Montessori teacher education courses. Susan has been writing about Montessori practice since the 1970's and this is her 14th Montessori book; many have been translated into other languages.

Susan has AMI Montessori graduate diplomas at 0-3, 3-6, and 6-12 levels, and has worked with adolescents; editing *The Erdkinder*, a newsletter documenting early exploration into the formation of the first farm school in the USA. She has degrees in philosophy, world religions, and education, and studied with Dr. Howard Gardner at the Harvard Graduate School of Education

In 2021 Susan was recognized for her work by GWI, *the Graduate Women International*, an international organization formed in 1918 in Europe to support the education of girls and women worldwide.

www.susanart.net

www.susanmayclinstephenson.net

BOOKS

The Joyful Child: Montessori, Global Wisdom for Birth to Three

This book truly reflects the spirit and purpose of Montessori in a way that makes the philosophy translatable to both new parents and veteran Montessorians. Susan's extensive experience and her world travels resonate as she explores the universal, emotional, and psychological depths that construct the child's development.

—Virginia McHugh, past Executive Director of The Association Montessori International USA (AMIUSA)

Child of the World: Montessori, Global Education for Age 3-12+

Stephenson's volume is a wonderful resource for parents seeking thoughtful, sound advice on raising well-grounded children in a chaotic world. Presenting Montessori principles in clear and eloquent prose, Stephenson's legacy will be a tremendous service to generations of parents to come.

—Angeline Lillard, PhD, professor of psychology, University of Virginia, author of *Montessori, The Science behind the Genius*

The Red Corolla, Montessori Cosmic Education (for age 3-6+)

In the section of this book on physics she shares how to do many science experiments, describing how to set up the science experiments and give presentations. The book also deals with botany, zoology, music, geography, art, and history. If 3-6-year-old children can experience as much as possible of these materials, they have created a lovely foundation for the Cosmic Education of the elementary years.

—Judi Orion, Director of Pedagogy and 0-3, 3-6 teacher trainer, Association Montessori Internationale (AMI)

The Universal Child, Guided by Nature, a Montessori Perspective

Simple, elegant, inspiring. Susan Stephenson carries Dr. Montessori's vision of education for peace forward with this lovely, simple book about what we can all recognize as universal in our make-up as human beings.

Those things that ought to (and can) bring us to a place of great respect for children through positive, intelligent engagement with them the world over.

—Gioconda Bellonci, Montessori parent and teacher

Montessori and Mindfulness

The author writes with such clarity and simplicity yet takes on the complexity of Montessori philosophy and contemporary thoughts on mindfulness with such grace and care. Her overall theme that personal fulfillment leads to care for others and for our environment echoes throughout each chapter and creates a wonderful symbiosis of Montessori thought and mindfulness practices, with personal stories throughout

—Lynne Breitenstein-Aliberti, Association Montessori Internationale, United States (AMIUSA)

No Checkmate, Montessori Chess lessons for Age 3-90+

I can wholeheartedly recommend this book. I had a child in my elementary class who was determined to teach every child to play chess. However she found it hard to slow down and would get frustrated that they could not just pick up the game after a simple explanation of what each piece does. I gave her your book from our class library and it significantly improved her chess teaching and also her relationship with others.

—Rachel Ammendsen, Dublin Ireland

Montessori Homeschooling, One Family's Story

Our English department teachers read Montessori Homeschooling, One Family's Story *and then made a presentation to all the Middle and High School staff. It was very impressive for the whole group of teachers. When* students recognize the purpose and are a fundamental part of what they are learning, they are more likely to dig deeper, and find ways to learn about what is important and relevant to them.

Teachers have come to nurture our students' desires and help them connect to their passions and interests.

—The English teachers, Montessori Colegio Bilingue, Cali, Colombia

Aid to Life, Montessori Beyond the Classroom

This is a wonderful book about Montessori and how it is being used in many countries. We will be translating it into French.

—Victoria Barres, Association Montessori Internationale representative to UNESCO, The United Nations Educational, Scientific and Cultural Organization. Paris, France

Please Help Me Do It Myself, Observation and Recordkeeping for the Primary and Elementary Class

Having been out of the classroom for two years, as I read this book I thought to myself "It is though I am in a refresher course". Thank you for writing this book.

—Adebanke Foloye, Nigerian AMI 3-6 and 6-12 Montessori teacher

I am a book club facilitator for our local Montessori organization, and we just finished a five-week study of Please Help Me Do It Myself. This is a fantastic book and we think it should be required reading in Montessori training centers. Such a great combination of theory and pragmatic ideas.

—Tara Valentine, Bay Area Montessori Association (San Francisco)

Brief Montessori Introductions Series

Montessori Cosmic Education

People often ask, "What did Dr. Montessori mean by Cosmic Education"? Susan Mayclin Stephenson has now given me a simple but profound way to answer this question. She does it in the very organization of the book. The first half is about key child developmental issues in the various age groups: Birth to 3, 3 to 6, and 6 to 12+. Then there is a little two-page chapter about making the world a better place. I read on and found my answer to Cosmic Education for each of those age groupings. In general Cosmic Education is an aide to help children find a place for themselves where they can develop and at the same time make the world a better place. The author is quite specific about the contributions of each of these age groups. She is offering an education that fosters ways from babies to adolescents to make good contributions for a better world. Parents and educators would benefit from this book, as I did.

—Rita Schaefer Zener PhD, AMI Primary Teacher Trainer

(new) *Beginnings, Montessori Birth to Three Comparison with Traditions in Bhutan*

(new) *The Music Environment for All Ages, Montessori Foundations for the Creative Personality*

The Universal Child Guided by Nature, a Montessori Perspective

10th Anniversary Edition

Michael Olaf Montessori Company
PO Box 1162
Arcata, CA 95518, USA
www.michaelolaf.net
michaelolafcompany@gmail.com

For translation and foreign publishing rights contact:
michaelolafbooks@gmail.com

More Montessori Information
www.montessori.edu

ISBN: 978-1-879264-35-9

Made in the USA
Monee, IL
14 March 2024

55049185R00069